ALL I NEED TO KNOW I LEARNED FROM MY CAT

ALL I NEED TO KNOW I LEARNED FROM MY CAT

By Suzy Becker

MY CAT

WORKMAN PUBLISHING · NEW YORK

Library of Congress Cataloging-in-Publication Data

Becker, Suzy.
All I need to know I learned from my cat / by Suzy Becker.
p. cm.
ISBN 0-89480-824-9 (pbk.)
1. Cats—Caricatures and cartoons. 2. Cat owners—Caricatures and cartoons.
3. American wit and humor, Pictorial. I Title.
NC1429.B3515A4 1990
741.5′973–dc20   90-50365
                                                                                                    CIP

Workman books are available at special discounts when purchased in bulk for premiums and sales promotions as well as for fund-raising or educational use. Special editions or book excerpts can also be created to specification. For details, contact the Special Sales Director at the address below.

Workman Publishing
708 Broadway
New York, NY 10003

Manufactured in the United States of America

First printing September 1990

30 29 28 27 26

For Amy
and my family.
AND BINKY

with special thanks to Ellie, Sally,
Annie and Peter for maki~ ~ book
possible. AND BINKY for e~ ~ ;IDEA
~~In~~ THis i ever hAd.

IT'S O.K. TO WEAR THE SAME THING EVERY DAY.

SLEEPING IS VERY UNDERRATED.

Detail

Never crack your knuckles.

SO IS STRETCHING.

GROOMING REQUIRES A SERIOUS TIME COMMITMENT.

REMEMBER TO WASH
BEHIND YOUR EARS,

IN BETWEEN YOUR TOES

AND UNDER YOUR ARMS.

KEEP YOUR NAILS TRIMMED,

NOTE: While the public
generally appreciate
good grooming —
they do n<u>o</u>t generally
appreciate it in public.

AND YOUR HAIR CLEAN.

PEE WITHOUT GETTING
ANY ON YOUR SHOES.

GET SOMEONE ELSE TO CLEAN YOUR BATHROOM.

EAT WHEN YOU'RE HUNGRY.

WHEN YOU'RE NOT HUNGRY, PLAY WITH YOUR FOOD.

IF YOU DON'T SEE IT, ASK FOR IT.

HAVE NO QUALMS ABOUT SHARING A PLATE

OR EATING LEFTOVERS.

DON'T BURP IN PUBLIC.

DRINK MILK.

Try not to obsess about cholesterol.

HELP WITH THE CROSSWORD.

BE HARD TO LEAVE.

NOTICE
THE SQUIRRELS.

CHASE
THE BUTTERFLIES.

INVESTIGATE THE SHADOWS.

MAKE YOUR OWN HOURS.

SHRED ALL DOCUMENTS.

MONEY'S ONLY PAPER.

BE CURIOUS.

GET TO KNOW PEOPLE IN HIGH PLACES.

DON'T BE AFRAID TO TAKE CHANCES.

TAKE A MOMENT
TO RECOVER YOUR DIGNITY.

BUT DON'T DWELL
TOO MUCH ON THE PAST.

DON'T ALWAYS COME WHEN YOU'RE CALLED.

TRY NEW THINGS.

Gloat.

TAKE SOME TIME TO EAT THE FLOWERS.

STARE UNABASHEDLY.

BE TOLERANT — BUT NOT OVERLY ACCOMMODATING.

GET MAD WHEN YOU'RE STEPPED ON.

FORGET THAT YOU WERE STEPPED ON.

KNOW ALL THE SUNNY PLACES.

SOMETIMES YOU CAN'T EXPLAIN YOUR ACTIONS.

SOMETIMES YOU CAN'T EXPLAIN YOURSELF.

HAVE A SNEEZE THAT'S THE ENVY OF OTHERS.

CHALLENGE YOURSELF.

SHARE YOUR VICTORIES.

RECYCLE

EXERCISE DAILY.

SEE A DOCTOR ONCE A YEAR.

PRETEND YOU'VE NEVER HEARD OF FLOSSING.

GO BAREFOOT

OBEY YOUR INSTINCTS.

CLAIM YOUR OWN CHAIR.

FLAUNT YOUR HAIR LOSS.

TAKE PRIDE IN YOUR WHISKERS.

DON'T PLUCK YOUR EYEBROWS.

VARY YOUR HANGOUTS.

MAKE THE WORLD YOUR PLAYGROUND.

RECOGNIZE THE TOY IN EVERYTHING.

MAKE THE MOST OF UNSTRUCTURED TIME.

THERE IS ALWAYS TIME FOR A NAP.

BE EASY TO COME HOME TO.

Diagram A:

6
3
1
4
2
5

SHOW AFFECTION,

AND CONTENTMENT.

HELP PUT THE GROCERIES AWAY.

EVERYONE IS ENTITLED TO AN OCCASIONAL MOOD SWING.

THE FASTER YOU RUN UPSTAIRS
THE MORE LIKELY YOU ARE TO FORGET WHY YOU WENT
IN THE FIRST PLACE.

THERE IS NOTHING WRONG WITH CHANGING YOUR MIND.

Time
elapsed   0:00   0:02   0:02½   0:03
(seconds)

AVOID COMPANY YOU DO NOT LIKE.

ACCEPT THAT NOT ALL COMPANY WILL LIKE YOU.

LOVE UNCONDITIONALLY.

DEPEND ON OTHERS WITHOUT LOSING YOUR INDEPENDENCE.

ENJOY YOUR OWN COMPANY.

BE A GOOD LISTENER.

INVITE YOURSELF TO DINNER.

SCRATCH WHEN IT ITCHES.

Don't drool.

GET USED TO SILENCES.

BE ENTERTAINING.

STRIKE POSES.

1.   2.   3.

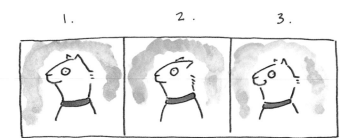

WIGGLE YOUR EARS.

JUMP RIGHT INTO THE MIDDLE OF THINGS.

JUST BECAUSE YOU'RE HOME,
YOU DON'T HAVE TO ANSWER THE PHONE.

FEEL NO GUILT.

Use negative attention-getting ONLY as a last resort.

ASK FOR ATTENTION.

IGNORE T.V..

YAWN LIKE YOU MEAN IT.

FIND A GOOD LAP TO CURL UP IN.

BE MYSTERIOUS.

BE ABLE TO MAKE
SOMEONE FEEL BETTER
BY JUST BEING THERE.

Walk softly.

MAKE PEOPLE WONDER WHAT YOU DO AT NIGHT.

BE GOOD AT FINDING THINGS IN THE DARK.

HAVE A WARM BED.

BE LOVED.

DREAM.